Essence
The Zen of Everything

Scott Shaw

Buddha Rose Publications

10 9 8 7 6 5 4 3 2 1

Printed in the United States of America

Essence

The Zen of Everything

Table of Contents

6

This book is not an attempt to tell anyone where it is at or how life truly is. It is simply a statement of how this person has witnessed things to be. Because of this reason, the understandings presented in this book are never truly completed, for with the ever-changingness of life, feelings and realizations, these words are just a small portion of the understandings of this person and an even smaller portion of the knowledge of all humanity.

Chapter I

Aphorisms 1975 - 1980

1

It is all what you make of it.

2

In a mechanical world there is mechanical
problems.

3

Help people and don't destroy anything.

4

Do the birds flying through the air worry about
enlightenment?

5

One can know a man by the shoes that he wears.

6

Was does not count.

7

It all goes back to mother earth.

8

Forcing causes resistance.

9

Extremes cause disharmony.

10

If you travel in the night you will miss the scenery.

11

If you go too fast there are accidents.

12

If you have high expectations, things rarely live up to them.

13

"If," is too big of a word for me.

14

Only when you let it.

15

When you cry you should leave one eye open to see the effect that you are having.

16

It is easy to find something to criticize.

17

Nothing lasts forever.

18

The builders always say, "I did it."
The destroyers always say, "I didn't do it."

19

Truth is the best thing you can give a person.

20

Guilt is the worst thing you can give a person.

21

Trust.

22

Friends need no contracts.

23

When it is over, it is over.

24

When you are in tune with nature and at peace with
yourself, you need no self-control or discipline.

25

Bad is what you make of it.

26

The more you scratch the more it itches.

27

You have to do something.

28

Things always seem better in memories.

29

There should never be a winner or a loser.

30

There are no definitions.

31

If things are straight and you rattle them, they become a mess.

If things are messed up and you rattle them, they become straight.

32

Headaches come from non-acceptance of a situation.

33

It is a wise person who knows when enough is
enough.

34

Clothing is changeable.

35

The truth always comes out.

36

Patience.

37

You do what you must.

That is the condition of this place we call life.

38

Do not make excuses for your indulgences.

39

Destiny is an excuse.

40

Simplicity is truth.

41

Life is simple if you make it simple.

Life is complex if you make it complex.

42

No one has the power to make you do something that you do not want to do.

43

Life is lived in moments.

44

Would you like to kill a cow, skin it, clean it, and cook it to eat your hamburger?

45

You can only worry about what you eat when times are good.

46

When you buy the ticket, you have to take the ride.

47

Money, it comes and goes.

When it is there, it can be spent.

When it is not there, there can be no spending.

48

Things come when they come.

49

Above all, be happy and peaceful.

50

Pleasure and pain are all what you make of them.

51

Inner strength is developable.

52

Inner strength is necessary.

53

Truth.

54

Discipline is kindergarten.

55

Does it really matter what others think?

56

If you are in a hurry and rush or if you are in a hurry and peaceful, the same things get accomplished.

57

One can remain innocent while not remaining naive.

58

Sometimes you just have to start things to see where you end up.

59

Careful choices are important.

60

Never do anything that may catch up with you and effect you negatively in the future.

61

The mind loves to worry and create problems where there are none.

62

Rejection causes friction.

63

Friction causes disillusionment.

64

Extremes cause disharmony.

65

The prophets in the time of Jesus said the world was coming to an end.

The prophets of today say the world is coming to an end.

Perhaps in two thousand years the prophets will make the same statement.

66

You can run or fight

       it is a personal choice.

67

There is happiness in usefulness.

68

Gamblers like to win but love to lose.

       Soldiers wish to live but long to die.

69

Nervous breakdowns are the easy way out.

70

Life is a paradox.

71

Wherever one goes to vacation,
        that too is someone's home.

72

You know when you know.

73

Sometimes aloneness brings loneliness.

        Other times it brings welcome solitude.

74

Nothing lasts forever.

75

To know peace you have to live it.

76

Things get done when they are done.

77

There is no hurry.

78

As the years go by, if you consciously observe
yourself you will understand your true nature more
and more.

79

Let yourself feel like the wind through the trees and the ocean waves.

80

There are many seekers

       but few knowers.

81

If you think you know,

       you never know.

82

All can know.

83

This reality we all know.

       Other realities are questionable.

84

Are other realities real or just somebody's fictional tale?

85

The mind thinks abstractly when it does not wish to deal with something.

86

One man's realization is not another man's
realization.

87

Realization is not something you get.

88

You cannot force realization.

89

No matter how much external stimuli is used,
realization is an inward process.

90

Self-actualization is not self-realization.

91

Self-actualization is more functional than self-
realization.

92

In realization, one does not all of a sudden know
God.

One all of a sudden knows themselves, which
becomes the essence of God.

93

To ascend to the higher realms seems so impressive.

Many strive all their lives to achieve this goal.

94

Do not run after out of body consciousness.

Instead, seek total body consciousness.

95

The word God is a name.

Names make an attempt at a definition.

Calling God a name takes away the true beauty.

96

God cannot be called him or her.

97

God may not save you from death just because you are religious, but with a mind turned towards God, you will go peacefully.

98

If you see God as good and evil as good, you are in heaven.

99

God is not only in one place.

God is everywhere, everything.

100

If you can look the embodiment of evil in the eyes and love it, the embodiment of evil becomes the embodiment of good.

101

If God is the total of everything, how could there be anything else?

102

Religion does not lead one to God, truth does.

103

Life is like a winding road at night. All you can do is follow the centerline.

104

In every moment, there is a fork in life's road.

You can either choose to go to the left or the right.

105

Those who search for enlightenment never find enlightenment.

106

Enlightenment does not mean knowing all.

It simply means understanding the essence of the mountains, the rivers and the energy that flows through them.

107

Yogis go insane can call it enlightenment.

108

Strict yogic practices are a great way to lose touch with reality.

109

Just be enlightenment.

110

To be able to reach down and drink out of a mountain stream, that is holy water.

111

The city breeds neurosis, discontentment, unhappiness, and loss of peace.

112

When it is a land of non-peace, there are many psychiatrists.

113

The worst thing that can happen is that you will die.

114

A man only pays for his sins once.

115

Stealing is stealing no matter what the reason.

116

Lying is lying no matter what the reason.

117

Lies are told to build ego or to keep one from hearing the true facts.

118

Sometimes people tell the same lie so many time that it becomes the truth.

119

Does a lie change the truth?

120

Attunement and closeness to nature brings peace.

121

Being close to nature, one knows meditation.

122

It is better to walk around something than to fight
your way through it.

123

Christianity, Hinduism, Buddhism. It is all religion.

124

Recovering from tragedy makes one more
appreciative of life.

125

If you feel love everywhere, personal love loses its
impact.

126

Some people are born to search for love.

Some people are born to turn away from love.

127

People break their own hearts.

128

If love is love, it never dies even when it is over.

129

Personal love is an empty box with its top closed.

130

In the end, you do not belong to anyone and no one belongs to you.

131

For some couples a relationship helps them grow,

      for others, it destroys them.

132

People make sex something that you get.

133

Sex is a momentary pleasure.

134

Sexual desire ceases when you achieve orgasm.

135

Do not be sorry.

      If you are going to be sorry, do not do it.

136

The body has a long list of needs: eating, drinking, and sleeping.

These basic needs are multiplied by a million due to personal desires.

137

Hold first times dear,

      for they are the most important.

But remember,

every time you do something is the first time.

138

Some people are born positive.

      Some people are born negative.

139

Some negative people try hard and become positive.

Some positive people try hard and become negative.

140

Embarrassment comes from allowing other to see all sides of yourself.

141

Anger is based in the fact of wanting things to be
different than they are.

142

By yourself, you can be yourself.

143

It is easy to can get caught up in the actions you are
expected to be doing.

144

It is all right to wonder.

145

Philosophy draws no answers.

       Experience leaves no doubts.

146

If you do not know by experience, you do not know.

147

Look and you will see.

148

You can experience things you have not known
through your dreams.

149

To identify peace,

> you must first know un-peace.

150

Be at peace.

151

All things come when they are needed.

152

Every moment is perfect and can never be lived again.

> So enjoy it, no matter what.

153

It is said, "Better to stop short than to fill to the brim.

Better to leave not quite full but wanting more."

But in truth, it is better to have your fill of something.

Then you are done with it and do not wish to return for more.

154

Technology is conquering earth.

It will conquer space, but you are the only one who can conquer yourself.

155

One cannot experience everything. If you did, your mind would explode.

156

Killing never helps anything.

157

One always desires what they cannot have.

158

Pleasure and pain are all what you make of them.

159

Good things always seem to end too fast.

160

No matter how much one argues the point, artificial intoxicants cause more problems than they answer.

161

Drugs lead to out-of-tunement.

They are not natural in the body nor does the body
need them.

162

Sometimes a little extra effort makes a lot better
work.

163

Music is like a Zen painting,

the silence between the notes is just as important as
the notes themselves.

164

There is no room for paranoia in mysticism.

165

Each person knows every other person in the world.

Each person has acquaintances and they have
acquaintances and so on. Thus, the entire world is
completely linked.

166

When you don't know what to do, don't do
anything.

167

Life is speculation.

Death is speculation.

168

Some things are better left unsaid.

Chapter II

Aphorisms 1981 - 1983

169

Everything is as it is.

170

When there is no movement,

        there is silence.

171

Life is full of compensations for what is truly
lacking.

172

The mind loves to justify compensations.

173

Life is lived by availability.

174

If you have to explain yourself, it is not worth
saying.

175

Even the newest clothing gets old and dirty
eventually.

176

Innocence is beauty.

177

You cannot miss when you have never known.

178

A philosopher always speaks negatively.

179

The unseen light is not light.

180

All things come when they come.

181

With no expectations,

       there can be no disappointments.

182

If something is too straight,

       it breaks instead of bending.

183

Who are you trying to impress?

184

Create!

185

Love is the most important thing one person can give to another person.

186

Lust gives one nothing.

187

If nothing is changed,

       there is no difference.

188

What is, is.

       What wasn't, never was.

189

To kill one life to save another is never worth it.

190

The more a hunter kills, the easier it becomes.

191

All things have the right to live.

192

Sacrifice is no sacrifice.

193

Nature moves in circles.

194

Nature defines the laws of this universe.

What is right will always be right.

What is wrong will always be wrong.

It does not change with culture, style, or time.

195

Ever notice nature is perfect?

196

Through science we come to understand that all of nature is striving for equilibrium.

Sometimes it is obtained.
Sometimes it is not.

When it is obtained, time moves on, change occurs, and eventually the equilibrium is lost.

Nature is once again set in motion seeking it.

This is the case of humanity, as well.

197

Nature is beautiful.

Animals are beautiful.

How can man kill simply to appease his taste buds?

198

Man has a reason for cutting and pruning trees,
nature does not.

199

People try to paint, sculpt, and photograph nature
but nature cannot be captured.

200

Watch yourself see.

201

If you create the situation, you have to live it.

202

When you make the rules, you have to play by
them.

203

Thoughts are demonstrated by actions.

204

When you finish with something, walk away from it
completely.

205

Remember, it is just someone to dance with.

206

Like a child at a baseball game who brings a
catcher's mitt, we all want to belong.

207

Most people just pass through their lives, leaving
nothing, living only the momentary pleasures and
pains.

208

Each person is born.   Many give birth to others.
Though a specific person may do nothing of
importance in their lifetime, somewhere, sometime
down the birth line, a child of importance will come
and that will make that distant ancestor's part
worthwhile.

209

The color of the ocean is just a reflection of the sky.

210

There are many vibrations in the atmosphere.

      If you let them, they all can affect you.

211

When something is mixed into the whole only once,
it bends with what is already there and will only
dissolve.

212

Much is lost in translations.

213

You can begin with religion,

      for one must start somewhere.

Put your faith in it and live it,

      but do not get caught up with it.

214

Do not take religion seriously.

215

How do we know what Jesus, Mohammed, or
Buddha said?

>What are recorded in the scriptures are
>recollections of disciples, not the actual
>writings of these men.
>
>How much of an accurate word-by-word
>description can you give of a conversation
>you had an hour ago? These remembrances
>were written years later.

216

The Bible is interesting.

In the Old Testament, they are awaiting the
Messiah.

In the New Testament, once they found him, they
immediately lose him and are awaiting his return.

His return and the end of the world are both
awaited.

217

Christians look at Greek mythology as nonsense.
Yet, look closely at the ideas of heaven, hell,
purgatory, limbo, God on a throne, Jesus by his
side, multi-headed monsters in revelations -- not
much of a difference.

218

Catholic priests learn how to read Latin because it is
believed to be holy. Why don't they learn to read
the ancient Hebrew Greek, and Aramaic -- the
languages in which the Bible was actually
compose?

219

The Christian religion was spread by means of
threats and death.

       Hardly the teachings of the Bible.

220

Christians criticize Hindus because they believe
they worship idols - namely the pictures and statues
of various deities. Yet, what adorns Christian
churches? Pictures of Jesus. Pictures of Mary. The
cross.   What is the difference?

People choose symbols to represent God.

221

Would Jesus have had light brown trimmed hair,
blue eyes, and clean white clothing?

222

Do you personally know that Jesus, the Buddha, or
Krishna existed?
Have you seen them?

223

Many psychotics believe they are the Son of God.

What makes Jesus and the other avatars so
believable?

224

Was the Buddha any more of a saint for leaving his
wife and unborn child than a man who reaches a
middle age crisis and seeks fulfillment outside of
his marriage?

225

Was Krishna right alluring and making love to the
wives of others?

226

Was Rama right in killing people?

227

Is it a valid religious belief that untouchables may
not read holy books and never be as good as others?

228

If one steps back from their religion and truly looks
at it, they begin to see the absurdity.

229

Religion creates structures that are not fair.

230

All religions make people feel guilty.

231

Religious people look at good times as a gift from
God and bad times as a test.

232

Modern religious people feel that they are much
holier than those who worship the rivers, the trees,
and the wind.

Yet, is worshiping these things that brought these
people life so non-understandable?

These things are much more finite than God.

233

New religions always offer new alternatives.

234

All religions:

Buddhism,
Christianity,
Hinduism,
Islam

expect worship.

235

Do not look for God.

God cannot be seen.

Do not try to touch God.

God cannot be felt.

Yet, all questions are answered, all desires granted,
and all truths prevail.

But God did not do it.

God is.
Truth is.
We are.
And, energy may be channeled.

236

God is the source-energy in all things.

237

Is God what you think God is or is God what God
is?

238

Trying to conceive of what God looks like is wrong.

God cannot be conceived.

239

Worshiping what you think God looks like, is worshiping false idols.

240

The reason people worship idols and pictures are because God cannot be seen.

   To worship God, there must be an image.

241

People continually refer to the ways or the laws of God.

God has no ways or laws.

These are only designed by mankind.

If God had laws, there would be no debate as to what was the true religion.

242

God does not become pleased or displeased.

243

God is not an individual looking down and judging each person.

244

Man judges man.
     God does not.

245

God is the energy flowing through out the universe,
in and of everything.

246

What makes a holy man a holy man?

247

Monks, priests, swamis, yogis, and nuns give up
sex, money, and material possessions in an attempt
to prove that they are above these things and are, in
fact, above the average person.
     The truth is they are not.
     They are human beings just like all of us.

248

Monks, priests, swamis, yogis, and nuns do not live
their life for God as they claim. They live their
lives based in ego.

Why do they wear specific clothing?

To demonstrate to the world that they are something
that others are not.

If they were truthfully living their lives for God,
clothing and titles would not be used.

249

Even the most enlightened person still has his or her
own human nature. They are still trapped in a
human body.

250

Being a priest, swami, yogi, or rabbi is something
that is earned.

       Being a holy man is not earned.

251

Holy is always holy.

       It has no name.
       No title.
       No specific type of clothing.

252

Many of the world's great spiritual teachers are
referred to as being above bodily consciousness.

If this were true, why did many of these holy beings
shave their face, trim their hair, or shave their
heads?

It seems if these people cared so little about bodily
things: mustaches, haircuts, or even shaved heads,
which depicted their sainthood, would not have
mattered.

253

In India, they believe a man to be enlightened because he goes into seizures and screams out to cosmic unseen images.

Enlightenment or insanity?

254

A yogi is a seeker of experience.

255

A yogi who has had so called enlightening experiences can say,

"I have had it, you have not."

256

One who sees a form or image of God in a vision has not seen God -- nor are they enlightened.

They are just fooling themselves.

God transcends image.

257

A monk who lives for many years in a cave or monastery cannot come out and deal with the normal stress and problems of society.

258

In most cases, people do not do austerities to be austere, but to bring attention to themselves.

From being noticed, they receive ego gratification.

The problem is they do not believe this to be the case.

Thus, they will never know true enlightenment.

259

If one worships a man as God, the slightest imperfection causes them to lose faith and become upset.

260

A spiritual teacher only teaches spirituality from his or her own point of view.

261

There are many teachers.

Some teach the truth, some do not.

Some become caught up in their own falsehood.
Some become caught in their own power.

Some teach simply for power and fame.

262

The true teacher does not claim to be a teacher.

263

The true teacher is silent.

264

The true teacher does not try to convert or change people.

265

The true teacher does not take on students.

266

The truth is lost when one thinks that they have become a teacher.

267

The world, its people, its promises, and prophecies pull one in many directions.

268

There is no teacher or teachings that can lead you to the truth of life after death, for once you die, the self is lost and teachings no longer matter.

269

If you cannot find something that lives up to your standards, it is better to leave that desire behind.

270

Your past didn't affect me.

My past didn't affect you.

271

A fantasy robs the beauty of the moment.

272

It is difficult for anything to ever live up to a fantasy,

for a fantasy is the perfect set of occurrences.

273

If you daydream too long about how something will be, it will never be as good as expected.

274

If you sees a certain place as home,

no new place can ever become home.

275

Make yourself at home.

276

To catch someone when they fall,

    you already have to be lower then them.

277

The only reason one gets upset in a traffic jam is
that they are in a hurry.

278

If a man doesn't think that he's a slave,

    then he is not a slave.

279

People measure their days by how much they have
accomplished,

not by how much more they understand.

280

Does a man who lives close to the earth and nature,
who eats what he grows, drinks the natural water
around him, become worried about money?

281

What is karma?

282

Karma is misunderstood.

283

The thinking mind tries to make karma scientific.

It is not.

284

People only view karma on the surface.

This person did that to me, so he will get his karma.

Most people never attempt to understand
why a person takes the actions that they
take.

Was it an individual action or influenced by family,
friends, or religion?

Was the action based in desire, faith,
psychology, or a reaction to environment, or
a childhood experience?

There are far too many variables to ever
think that you can understand or chart
karma.

285

When a person is stressed or upset, they think
upsetting thoughts.

286

All things involving life and nature flow in cycles,

      from hair growing to creativity.

287

Work is not God's only plan.

288

If you want something long enough,

      you will get it.

289

Think of the other person first.

      What effect will it have on them?

290

If you have to cry,

      it was not worth it.

291

If you understand the truth, then there is no need for rules.

Why? Because you already know what is right or wrong.

292

When you pray for an object and receive it, this is
not because God has answered your prayers -
though the purveyors of religion tell us this is the
case.

The reason the object appeared is two fold:

One, you desired it.

So, when it appeared, it was appreciate.

If you didn't want it, you would not care that it had
arrive

Two, you have put so much energy into your desire,
that the energy of attraction has brought it to you.

293

Energy is channelable.

294

The people one associates with will influences their
lives.

295

Impression only lasts for an impressionable amount
of time.

296

The human mind thinks that it is the center of the universe, just as the ancient Greeks thought that the earth was the center of the universe.

297

You do not have to like everything.

298

To truly not care about something that you have loved, you must first tire of it.

299

Just because you like something does not mean that you should not give it up as a means of spirituality austerity.

300

Are you willing to give it all up?

301

Experience.

302

Everything in the universe is interrelated.

303

The first law of thermodynamics states,

"No energy in the universe can be created or destroyed."

304

Each day, take some time for yourself.

305

Most people have nothing to truly believe in.

They do not believe in themselves.
So, they turn to an abstract concept like religion.

306

A person either becomes a functioning part of this world or they must leave it.

307

All desires are self-created.
   Once they are created, they grow.

308

   No ego,
   no desire,
   no thought,
   no self.

   Then, no body.

309

Sometimes you are just not going to get satisfaction
out of a situation.

It is better to just let go than to make yourself upset
wishing it had turned out a different way.

310

If you are going to teach someone something that
you have learned from someone else, do not teach it
until you have mastered it.

By teaching something that you have not yet
mastered, you create more problems than you solve.

311

People theorize about reincarnation and heaven due
to their longing for eternal life.

312

In the universe, no energy is created or destroyed,
just as there is no birth or death.

Only a moment with the knowledge of life.

313

There is no definition of spirituality,
        as there is none of nature,
                but man still tries to locate one.

314

Slow down.

315

Everything comes when it is needed.

    We decide what to do with it.

316

If you have done all you can in life and all of your creations of the moment have been completed, then you can die in peace at any time.

317

One should never suggest to another person that they should do something.

    For if you are wrong, they hate you.

    If you are right, they envy you.

318

If you are looking at something, you are judging it.

If you are living it, you are not judging it.

319

If it starts from a lie,

    it can never be the truth.

320

If you have to fix it to make it right,
it was already broken and not worth the effort.

321

Physical and material influences hide beneath the
surface.

      Spiritual influences are on the surface.

322

If you believe in superstition, it can affect you.

If you have to think whether or not you believe,

      then, you already believe.

323

By confining yourself to the physical world, you are
forced to live in it.

324

Everything has a reason.

325

If you do not know why, then you do not know.

326

If it is sensitive, it will hurt.

327

Does a slave choose to be a slave?

328

Jump from any coast and you will go to the bottom of the ocean.

329

One does not need to become structured to become unstructured.

330

Creativity is the highest good.

331

When one is spending all their time doing things that they do not wish to do, creativity is lost.

332

Loss of creativity is a loss of God.

333

To try and paint a picture of something that is, is a waste of time.

     For photographs do a much better job.

     But to paint feelings, that is art.

334

The simpler and freer a picture becomes, the more it becomes art.

335

The simpler and freer a life becomes, the more it becomes art.

336

Do the things that need to be done and be creative.

337

Creativity abounds in a land where a person's mind does not have to be focused upon politics.

338

Creativity abounds in a society where a person does not have to work for an employer who is getting rich off their labor.

339

There is not much room for creativity in a communist country.

340

There is a difference between a painter and an artist.

341

The artist does what he must to be creative.

342

It is very easy to talk about art.

It is very easy to give your opinion of what you have been programmed into liking and disliking, and what you believe to be beautiful.

But, opinions have nothing to do with true art.

Art is either present in a person's life or it is not.

Very few people are artists.

343

Studying art in scholastic institutions in the forms of art history, art theory, art philosophy and even supervised creative classes can never give one the experience of art.

> Art cannot be put into a book.
> Art cannot be graded.
> Art cannot be taught.
>
> Art must be lived to be understood.

344

To read of another man's artistic frustration,
depression, and insanity sounds so romantic and
creatively necessary.

Does it feel that way to that person?

345

If one desires a vision long enough, they will see
what they want to see.

346

When you start something,

you should finish it.

347

Man studies the universe with the hope of
understanding it.

When he understands it, he will want to change it.

Can any change man makes in nature, be a good
one?

Look what has happened so far.

348

If man destroys the earth,

the universe will still go on.

349

When one hears the age of the earth and sees how
one hundred years is but a microsecond, one knows
how little one's life truly matters.

350

Man's reasoning mind makes all things scientific.

> Heaven and Hell.
> This is a sin. That is not a sin.
> This is good karma. That is bad karma.

Go beyond all the sciences. Then you are free.

352

To say it is one's duty or destiny to die is a lie.

353

You cannot feel someone else's pain.

354

Whenever you interact with someone, karma is
created.

355

If you are not proud of everything that you do, then
do not do it.

356

Never sacrifice your morals or your standards for anyone.

> For then you will never have to feel anger at the person for whom you sacrificed them for.

357

If you can not tell everyone in the world what you have done,

> then do not do it.

358

Making love is the closest two people can be on the physical level.

359

To obtain the maximum enlightening experience from sex, there should be no thought or focus on the partner during orgasm.

Instead, your consciousness should be locked in the spiritual realms.

> This is not all that easy, however.

For it is the sexual partner who is giving you this mystical glimpse.

360

During orgasm, you can either think of your partner or embrace the cosmic nothing.

If you think of your partner, it feels good.

If you think of nothing, you get a glimpse of the absolute.

361

When two people have very good sex, it keeps them bound to the physical plane.

Thus, transcendence cannot occur.

362

To masturbate with no though of sex, doing it solely for the purpose of raising your consciousness, can be a truly purposeful experience.

But, if you have any thought of a fantasy partner, the spiritual experience is lost.

363

If there is a thought, total orgasm is not experienced.

364

After a person has had sex a few times, they begin to measure and compare the experience.

How good was it this time, compared to the last time?

With this, sex loses all of its Tantric, enlightening qualities.

It becomes simply a calculation of satisfaction and gratification.

365

If you are thinking whether a particular orgasm was good or not,

> how good could it have been?

366

The reason people become bored with sex and seek new partners is over time, the known becomes expected. But, the mind always remembers the newness and sensation of infatuation.

> Infatuation is a powerful drug.
> It is remembered and sought after.

367

Unconscious sex makes one lose respect for the partner because they become simply an object.

368

Sexual desire is natural.

Yet, at the moment after orgasm, there is a space of no desire.

This is the source-point for Tantric enlightenment.

369

It is the general consensus that when people first become sexually active, post the experience, they wonder, "Was that it?"

Time and technique may change this but this initial feeling demonstrates to a person the true illusion of sexual desire.

370

When orgasm means nothing, the time has come to give up sex.

371

If one has never experienced sex, nothing is being given up by being celibate.

372

If people did not regard sex as the most precious
thing to the body, it would not matter so much.

373

Once you are lovers, there is always ego
attachment. It is very hard to be friends.

374

The need to be with a partner is developed.

375

When people, live good,
            eat good,
            love good,
            have all the things they want,
            they do not wonder why.

376

You can only back yourself so far up against a wall.

377

As the world gets louder, people try to shut it out.

378

Does security come from what is outside or what is
inside?

379

There is a fine line between selfless service and
being taken advantage of.

380

Just because people do not know the truth about you
does not mean that it does not exist.

381

"Why" is the answer.

382

When you are close to the ocean, you hear each
individual wave. When you are farther away, you
hear only the roar.

383

It is best not to rush around through life and go to
sleep exhausted and strained. It is better to
gradually slow down, take it easy, and then slowly
drift into sleep.

384

Live the way that brings you peace.

385

Just because one is old and experienced does not
necessarily make them knowledgeable or good.

386

Age does not equal necessary wisdom.

387

By merging the many, you lose the truth of the one.

388

Sometimes you cannot explain to people how you feel or why you are doing what you do.

>   You can only be who you are.

389

There is no wind through the trees in a treeless forest.

>   Think about where you live, how you live, and what affect you life is having on this planet.

390

When death is a far easier journey than life, you are living in the wrong world.

391

Sometimes it is better to leave things until the morning.

392

Insecurity is the source of jealousy.

393

Weapons are for the man of war.

394

Animals eat other animals because it is their nature.

They do not have the ability to make a choice.

      Man does.

395

It is not hard for a person who has never eaten meat to be a vegetarian.

396

To a cannibal, eating other people is expected.

397

Death is death, no matter what the reason or cause.

398

Each of us needs something to do.

What it is we each chose to do is a personal choice.

But, without something to do, you lose yourself.

399

The actions of an anti-movement are dominated by
the group they are against.

400

Attachments go deep.

401

The longer one is with someone or something the
more attached they become, be it good or bad.

402

Most of our actions, our likes, our dislikes, are
psychologically based.

403

When one lies about a subject for a long period of
time, sometimes that lie becomes the truth.

404

All nature is striving for balance.

Man is the only creature of nature that prefers to
strive for material gains.

405

Right and wrong is defined by culture.

406

What is the cause of desire?

407

Is cold in itself a thing or is it just the lack of warmth.

408

Abstract ideas are much easier to think of than realist thoughts.

409

When one is upset, the entire world seems upset.

When one is peaceful, one cannot understand why anyone would be anything but peaceful.

410

Some people see the price $9.99 and think ten dollars. Others see it as nine dollars.

411

Many people have an ideal.

412

As long as it is finite, it is do-able.

413

The universe,

      by scientific definition, is finite.

414

Do you owe them a justification?

415

Come to understand what you do well,

      and then do it well.

416

People who grow up in poor countries desire material wealth.

People who grow up in rich countries desire material wealth.

Only the truth seeker desires things that have no material value.

417

There is no such thing as philosophy.

      Either you know or you do not know.

418

The middle path is a waster of time.

      You either do something or you do not do it.

419

A person only knows the distance between two places if he walks it.

420

If weight is on a scale, it will be weighed.

421

Seek out your own truth and live it, but make no one else live it.
422

Associating with a group to gain enlightenment is not the ultimate good, as many teachers of enlightenment proclaim.

In a group, the truth and experience of the individual is lost and the general acceptance of the group's common truth is all that remains.

423

When you see it everyday,

      anything becomes commonplace.

424

Take one hour each day to do nothing.

You will come to understand the essence of life.

425

Life is all you can live.

426

Observe the trends.

427

A profitable life, both spiritually and economically, is based in proper anticipation of the trends.

428

Symptoms are deceiving.

429

No guarantees.

430

Sometimes one must talk negatively about a subject in order to get a person's attention to listen to the positive.

431

All things serve their purpose.

432

If you are saying, "This is it," it is not.

433

Sometimes silence is the best word.

Chapter III

Aphorisms 1984 - 1989

434

Balance.

435

You are not caught in anyone else's illusion but your own.

436

Life is based on individual perception.

437

Feelings are your choice.

438

Sin translated from Latin means to join.

439

Yoga means yoking or union.

440

Observe.

441

Good or bad is a point of view.

442

All things take time.

443

The only sad thing about bubbles is that they pop.

444

A bird in the hand is worth two in the bush.

But, with a bird in the hand, there is no chance for new experience.

445

That is what you think?

      So what.

446

You can only choose when there is a choice to be made.

447

Choice is an illusion of the thinking mind.

448

When there is more than one to choose from,

      a decision must be made.

449

What you have to choose from is,

    what you have to choose from.

450

The funny thing is,

    it all just doesn't matter.

451

The amateurs make excuses for why they could not.

    The professional needs to make no excuses.

452

It takes a lot longer to realize something on your
own than to have it taught to you.

453

Witness the change.

454

More and more of this world is becoming the same.

    Soon every one will speak one language,
        dress alike,
           look alike.

    There will be only one culture, one race.

455

People speculate where the next war will occur.

How sad is it that the mind of man focuses
on such foolish things.

456

The world is full of lies.

In America, they believe India to be all holy.
In India, they believe all Americans to be all
wealthy.

457

You cannot appreciate what you have never tasted.

458

There is always something you can want.

459

Lie-brary

460

Desirable objects are easy to look at.

461

"Almost" means that you did not.

462

You should take time to slow down.

463

With nothing to do, you have the chance to dream.

464

Push back the frontiers of the unknown.

465

Someday you will exist only in memory.

466

There are moments of embarrassment in everyone's life that when you look back you can still feel the humiliation.

How long will you hold on to those feelings that have no value?

467

That is all very nice but "Before" is never coming back.

468

If that particular desire you have is answered, you will simply develop another one.

469

If that negative experience did not happen to you,
would you be as wise as you are today?

470

In a war, the opposing army will often times charge
the front lines then quickly retreat further back than
they were originally. Thus, causing the opposing
army to follow in chase where an ambush is
awaiting.

471

To win a battle, does it make you the better person
or simply a fool for entering into it?

472

Man loves to enforce his superiority in any situation
that he can.

Be it: power, knowledge, or wisdom.

In all cases, the superior eventually losses.

473

People always seek to gain power over one another.

474

Worldly people do certain things.

Spiritual people do certain things.

475

How much of our lives do we live for other people?

476

One sees only a reflection of the world.

477

The world can never truly be known.

It can only be experienced.

478

One can only see what there is to see.

479

For those who seek no truth,

they are not concerned with not finding it.

480

If you do not ask for guidance, you will receive none.

481

Most people do not want to know.

482

You do you pay the price?

483

Which is sadder, believing people are your friends,
when they are not or simply not having any?

484

People do not care what tears they cause.

485

Offering to rescue a person from his or her own
folly is never appreciated,

it only creates resentment.

486

Most people believe everything that they hear.

487

When one is given a gift, they smile and pretend
that they like it,

whether or not they do.

488

The older a person gets, the deeper their convictions
and ideals become, and the harder they are to
change.

489

Some people seek answers where there are none.

Some people do not care about answers.

Who is more holy?

490

You take two dogs, place them in a back yard and make them live together.

       Is your life much different?

491

The world is a trap.

Poor people cannot afford to buy new things. Thus, they purchase old used items, which continue to break, and they must continually invest money to keep them working.

       Money is spent.
       No money can be saved.
       People remain poor.

492

This is reality. Love it or leave it.

493

Life is inconsistent.

Death is consistent.

One who is consistent is dead.

494

One has to master complexity to understand simplicity.

495

Understand the subtleties.

496

Infinity is finite.

497

How strong is your shadow?

498

How does water know when it is hot enough to boil?

499

Second class or first class; you get there all the same, but it is all how you get there.

500

While traveling, one is forced into unfamiliar
circumstances, which is a cause of pressure.

501

When you see or experience new things, the
emotions are in flux.

502

The pressures of traveling: where to go, how to get
there, what to eat.

It is amusing if one can see it as much.

503

Modern society attempts to find a definition and
justification for everything, but when all of their
answers still leave questions, society will realize
that past the point of definition, there is no
definition.

504

First the definition must be known,

       then the no-definition can be understood.

505

If you wish to truly understand something, you must
go in one side of it and come out the other.

506

Have you ever thought of changing your mind?

507

It does not matter how well you do, as long as you do what you do with style.

508

The point is not how far or fast that you go. The purpose is how good you feel getting there.

509

If you can just get away from anticipation, then you will be free.

510

It is amazing how people get so caught up in their own momentary reality.

511

People are always making up excuses for their actions, reasons for the way that they are and what they are doing. They do not realize that these are not the truth, simply justifications.

512

The reason things do not get accomplished is that people are afraid to make the first step.

513

The first step is the hardest step.

514

It is always difficult to step into the abyss alone.

515

Everything just happens when it happens, so sit back and enjoy the waiting.

516

One can do what ever they want in life. The outcome is not important, but the doing gives one purpose.

517

Now people live longer, are more educated, have more wealth. And, as travel has become easier, and communication more accessible, one is more exposed to the vast array of world cultures. Thus, one has greater choices and larger opportunities.

But we still all will die.

518

All ecosystems seek equilibrium. The human species, now that it has been globally exposed, is currently seeking a global/human balance.

519

These are not simple times.

520

Today isn't yesterday.

521

The greatest thing about beauty is that it is so impermanent.

522

Do you seek your beauty in the eyes of others?

523

If there were no one to perform to, fame would mean nothing.

524

Decide for yourself.

525

One of the keys to life is to not make things too obvious.

526

Even if you don't have it, you should act like you do.

527

People never think what it costs the other person.

528

You have to know what to look for to see what you have to see.

529

Emotionally and psychologically, what does it do to a cat when it brings a dead mouse to your door and you scream at it? The cat thought it was giving you a gift.

530

Where does a gust of wind end?

531

Titles are for the ego-filled.

532

The average person sees another and judges them to be either superior or inferior to themselves.

533

One can say it a million times that all people are equal. It is human nature however, to believe this is not to be so.

People choose to believe that either they are greater or that others are superior to themselves in terms of wealth, power, fame, knowledge, and spirituality.

534

There is nothing one can do. The majority of people are egotistical and judgmental and see things only from their own point of view.

535

People do not have the ability to think for themselves. They are programmed to merge into the framework of the functioning culture and society.

It is for this reason that genius is most often called insanity and a visionary is titled a fool.

536

Sometimes a puppeteer lets go of the tension on the puppets strings and the puppet is allowed to dangle free for a time. The puppeteer pulls the strings tight again and the puppet performs.

537

The small-minded wants all to be the same.

538

People are either paired or in competition.

539

People imprison themselves in what they know.

They then cannot break out of it because they are afraid to move into the unknown.

540

Words are interpreted by individual definitions.

541

What is the source of words?

542

Language is simply memorization.

543

If one cares, they hold on. If one holds on, they never get anywhere new.

544

To forget, let everything pass through you.

545

Paying your dues is for someone who is in debt.

546

How many of our actions are done for ourselves and how many of them are motivated by the desire to seek the approval of others?

547

The potter makes the cup empty. It is the man who chooses to fill it with desired preference.

548

Spelled out conditions come from an understanding of the self or a clear definition of needs.

549

When one has to go to church early on Sunday, it is hard to stay out and party on Saturday night.

550

When one is finished with something, they throw it away.

How many times has something again been needed once it has been discarded?

551

One envisions their fantasies towards things and people known and seen.

552

Desire likes and desire dislikes.

553

Desire or necessity?

   It is all a point of view.

554

Desire is a fool's cup of tea.

555

Desire is money. Desire is power. Desire is sex.
Desire is God.

Desire just the same.

556

When one has a desire, they put a lot of energy into
obtaining it. When they achieve it, they have no
energy left to say thank you.

557

If a person desires something to be accomplished,
they set out to achieve it, with no regard for what it
may cost others, who may be directly or indirectly
involved. If one points this out to that person, they
become angry, feeling that their right to obtain that
desire is being hindered.

558

With thinking, comes desire.

559

Fulfillment equals desires met for a specific period of time.

By its very nature, it cannot be eternal.

560

Desires are free (no charge).

The price is paid later, when you set out to achieve them or have them in your grasp.

561

"I want this." "I do not want that." How much of our lives and feelings are dominated by these two statements?

562

If you have no needs, then all needs are answered.

563

How does a warrior exist when he no longer choose to be a warrior?

How does a mystic exist when he realizes the illusions of this world?

564

It is hard to be proud of a Sergeant's rank in the company of Generals.

565

Interaction brings about conformity.

566

Truth is only a perception, a limited point of view.

In the end one realizes nothing really matters anyway. So, a lie or a truth, it is all the same.

567

You are taught to believe something.

That says it all.

568

A fact is not necessarily the truth.

569

Is it a lie that you are telling yourself?

570

Is your wisdom riding back seat to your lust?

571

Live simply/simply live.

       Two statements.
       Two words each.

       It is for you to choose.

572

Simplicity without being simplistic.

       That is the key to this world.

573

If you know your own desire(s), at least that is a start.

574

When you walk away from something with pride, victory, or attainment, you can never walk back into it, for it is much harder to walk away form it with that same feeling the second time.

575

There are no saints with suntans.

576

If it were acceptable to cry in public how many people would be in tears?

577

When life is well planned and defined, there are no ups and downs. That is fine, but there is little experience gained as well.

When life is left to chance, there are turbulences. Here is where enlightenment is found.

578

Think of all the dreams and fantasies that people are now having and will have in the future.

Where do they all go?

579

One can only know what they know. Everything else is simply imagination.

580

Don't make excuses.

Time it is to short.

581

With one's eyes open they can learn, but only may also become distracted.

582

Passion costs money.

583

Don't concentrate on the problem. Concentrate on the solution.

584

Truth is a relative issue.

585

Who holds you into eternity?

586

One must never rely on what they have previously known. They must let each new situation teach them.

587

The saddest thing about life is that it is so short and it takes so much time to gain wisdom and knowledge. Then there is so little time left to put one's final knowledge to good use.

588

People always want others to suffer their misery or live their happiness.

589

People will always advise one from their own point of view.

590

What is the best in the world?

591

The Devil of this world is power.

592

The chief disciples of the Devil are the rich, the successful, the strong, the intelligent, the famous, and the beautiful.

593

This world loves to worship the Devil and his disciples.

594

Is a spiritual teacher successful and powerful?

595

The winner of a competition is obviously a follower of the Devil.

The loser of a competition is obviously a follower of the Devil.

596

Competition breeds desire.

597

There is no pride in victory, only a fool's reward.

598

Who is to say what is better or worse?

599

Better should be chosen over the lesser. Why take second best.

600

There are no mistakes.

601

All is simply as it is.

602

The beginning, the middle, and the end are all as they should be.

603

If one loves all circumstances, then one sees that there is no excuses, no mistakes, only perfection.

604

One cannot anticipate spiritual progression; one simply has to live it.

605

Swim up stream like the trout. Get where you are
going and die.

Flow with the river down stream. End up in the
vast ocean full of possibilities.

606

There is no such thing as being out of the flow, off
the path, or lost. These things are only states of
mind and excuses one makes for their own
inadequacy, in taking responsibility for themselves.

607

Most people who have gone down in history as
great did not keep detailed explanatory diaries or
journals. For if they had, the world would have
known their intimate thoughts, problems, and
desires. Then it would have been understood that
they were only human, not great.

608

The worst thing that a person can ever do to himself
or herself is to have a preconceived notion about a
subject and decide that they wish to learn nothing
about it.

609

Money, prestige, and power are everything in this
world. With out the need for them, most crimes and
induced pains would not be committed.

610

Strength is based in the opponent's fear.

611

Outward strength does not give prestige.

612

Pride does not come from power.

613

All power is temporal power.

614

If you place yourself in a world of competition,
there will always be someone stronger than you.

615

When you instigate a fight, argument, or discussion,
they immediately have placed them self in the
dominant position, for they are prepared.

The best defense is to not contend and withdraw.

The person who creates these confrontations then
feels that they have won. In fact, they are simply
the fool driven by their ego.

One should never take to heart points that are driven
home at these times of susceptibility.

616

In anger and in pleasure a thousand lifetimes can be
lived in a few short moments.

617

Anger and violence are emotions. Begin through
external stimulation. Being emotions, without
continued incentives, they will face away.

618

People become lost in momentary anger and then
are imprisoned by its outcome, due to the fact that
they do not realize the temporariness of that specific
feeling and emotion.

619

People place too much importance on the emotions
of the moment.

620

Ninety-eight percent of what we say and do is the
product of momentary emotion.

621

If you let your emotions run away with you, they
will run away with you.

622

Emotions are emotional.

623

Generally, a person does not realize that life has no meaning until they are about to die. Some realize it at a very old age and never understand it. Those who realize it at a young age become mystics, but then they are forced to live in a world that they see as only an illusion.

624

Life just gets ridiculous some where along the line.

625

Energy saved is energy waiting to be spent.

626

If you watch time, time watches you.

627

If you are going to bring a person from a distant place, be sure that you have more to offer where you are taking them than where they came from.

628

Curiosity is only skin deep.

629

Forgetting is an illusion. It is simply a way to pretend that something did not happen and thereby not come to terms with it.

630

If one cannot do something, they often take pride in their inability.

631

One either has to work at making their dreams come true or make their dreams work.

632

Tools only work if you know how to use them.

633

The end comes hard, but the truth comes easy.

634

If you compare yourself,

    you will always fine someone better.

635

Availability increases desire.

636

With availability comes usage.

637

With usage comes exploitation.

638

In general, modern people are inconsiderate.

639

Does a rock choose to be a rock?

640

When does a rock stop being a rock?

641

In some ways a photograph does capture the soul.

642

Sometimes it is better at a glance.

643

You can hear it, you can read it, but the truth is, no one can teach you anything. You must learn it for yourself.

644

People speak a lot about brotherhood, satsang, proper association, but when it comes right down to it, everybody is out for themselves.

645

The difference between the average person and a philosopher is that the philosopher records their findings.

646

Is consciousness an illusion?

647

How much time is spent in fantasy?

Virtually everything everyone thinks involves dreams, fantasies, and future desires.

648

Life, philosophy, God, and death are all speculation. Some just know how to formulate their speculations better.

649

Where does causation begin? Some say with the original sin.

Was the original sin not a choice and thereby influenced, as all choices are, by psychological, social, and environmental conditions.

650

Why should anything be the way someone says it should be.

651

Is traditional knowledge always right?

652

Science is only sure of one thing.

What is correct today will be proven wrong
tomorrow.

653

All the socio, ethnic, and culture studies you can do
mean nothing. For eventually there will only be one
culture.

654

Man, as his technologies have grown and
knowledge increased, has lost the ability to
appreciate the simplistic.

655

The sky is like nature's television set.

Everyday, every moment it changes.

 It is ever the same.

656

Nature knows its destiny.

657

Water is never at rest.

The river flows to the sea, the ocean feeds the clouds with evaporation, and then they rain onto the ground again.

658

Living in a situation where there is noise, as natural as it may be, one is continually distracted.

Living where there is silence, one is allowed to become introverted and study their own thoughts, situations, and ideas.

659

If you continually think about time, it goes by so much faster.

660

If you are forever in a hurry, time passes quickly.

661

When you slow down, time will slow down.

662

Time is for the dreamers.

663

Time should not be wasted.

664

A person who rushes through life hoping that soon they will have time to slow down finds a life quickly spent.

The opposite is true of a person who savors each moment and experiences it fully.

665

When you do things in your time, when you get around to it, it is not a gift to another person, though that may have been your intention. For you are giving when you feel like it and then it is no longer meaningful to another.

666

They come/they go.

667

What is low?

668

Who is high?

669

Saying thanks is not the same as giving thanks.

670

Observation is the beginning of the remedy.

671

A person who is made to serve others seeks to make others their servants.

672

With age comes technique.

673

The problem with a little illusion is that it often turns into a lot.

674

If you can't sleep in a noisy atmosphere, turn the sounds into visions in your dreams.

675

There is no such thing as pure or impure thoughts. Thoughts simply are thoughts.

676

The reason there is no right or wrong, pure or impure thinking is that this would mean that man has the ability of infinite judgment.

677

Culture creates right and wrong, pure and impure,
and culture creates thoughts.

678

If one wishes to control their thoughts, one must
trace them back to their source.

679

Here can never be there.

680

Prayer equals desire.

No desire. Prayer is not necessary.

681

No desire, no destiny.

682

The wise man desires
        no power,
        no fame
        and no love.

                How few they are.

683

To consciously be nothing is different from ending up as nothing.

A worldly person tries to be something and may end up as nothing and then despises all humanity. The mystical person realizes that the material world has nothing of permanence to offer and so chooses to be nothing, thus setting himself or herself free.

684

Beauty is simply another phrase for the desires of passion.

685

The longing and reason of one moment never seems to last into the next.

686

First, know your limitations, and then learn to work around them.

Then it will seem as if there are no limitations.

687

Memories are clear to the mind.

Future visions are unclear.

688

All things are seen through a limited perspective.
689

Opinions. Do they really matter?

690

Opinions are not actions.

691

Sometimes one looks for feelings and there simply
is nothing there.

692

You do not have to like something to accept it.

693

People speak of their happiness when another
succeeds or wins, but they actually prefer to witness
one fail or lose. For then they feel no competition
or comparison to themselves.

694

People love to speak of things that have no
meaning.

695

There is becoming a world society.

 This world society is wiping out regional culture.

696

In restaurants, Americans eat with chopsticks to show how worldly and cultured they are.

Asians just eat with them.

697

Asians eat with forks, knife, and spoon to demonstrate how cosmopolitan they are.

Westerners just eat with them.

698

People plant themselves like trees, often times in places which they do not even like and never move, never leave, spending their entire life in agony.

699

Complexity is where interest is born.

700

Simplicity is where boredom is born.

701

Doing nothing is still doing something.

702

No reason is the best reason.

703

Have you left yourself a moment to dream?

704

The minute water touches something it begins to evaporate.

That is the perfect description of life.

705

Memories are created by experiences.

706

Time goes by, measured only by the memorable moments.

707

Losing is easy.

Winning is much more difficult.

That is why the untrained mind prefers to lose.

708

My observations may be different than yours.

Yours may be different than mine.

All have different perspectives.

709

It takes a hundred positive expressions to equal the saying of one negative expression.

710

Fulfillment is an illusion.

711

When people have no greatness of their own, they bask in the greatness of others.

712

Today's realizations are tomorrow's false facts.

713

It is almost amusing how doing the mundane, the practical, the necessary in this world appears as accomplishment, when in fact, it achieves nothing at all.

714

If you have the opportunity to do something, do it
for the opportunity may never come again.

715

You have never been up until you have first been
down.

716

The world, its ways, and its financial requirements
has people so under control that all they generally
want to do when they are finished with a day of
labor is go home and relax. This is why so few
people anymore may be thought of as artists,
philosophers, or thinkers because they have no time
or energy for creative or spiritual vision.

717

Money dominates space.

718

People become addicted to external experiences.

Have you had enough yet? If you have, you can
just sit back and be quiet for a time.

719

The traditional educational system is ridiculous.
Textbooks are meant to be read, memorized, and
then they are forgotten. No one is taught how to
think for himself or herself.

720

Memorized knowledge is not understanding.

721

Yesterday's textbooks are discarded cheaply.

722

One is never complete.

> There is always more to learn.

723

There is no such thing as holy.

724

Life is man's folly.

> One shouldn't blame it on God.

725

Religion and culture go hand in hand.

726

Culture is based in religion.

Religion is based in culture.

727

It is okay to believe in nothing.

728

The more knowledge man gains, the more he loses superstition and religion.

729

Man on the whole is turning away from religion and morality.

Good or bad, this is the case.

730

All teachings are valid. Some are just more ornamented than others.

731

A Messiah is only a man.

732

What makes a man a Messiah?

People believe him to be one.

Then when he dies, many stories are invented and claims are made that miracles were seen.

733

Some say that a Messiah does not die but simply leave their body.

Yet, the body dies.

A man is only man

And, has any Messiah ever returned that you know about?
734

Jesus committed suicide.

Had he chosen to be silent, he would not have been crucified.

735

Missionaries make such a big deal of how they converted native groups over to their religious beliefs.

But, let's face it; converting uneducated, simple, superstitious people is not such a great accomplishment.

736

I would not call it prophecy but rather insightful
good sense when who ever wrote the Bible
predicted that one power would eventually rule the
world.

Just as in nature,
         the human species is seeking equilibrium.

737

To think of religion is not to live religion.

738

Christianity is so well organized that if you talk
badly about it or if you don't believe what it
teaches, you will go the worst place that anyone can
imagine: hell.

Good marketing ploy, yes?

739

To Christians, the thought of Satan is like paranoia.

But, there is nothing really there.

740

The Christians have this foolish belief that the soul is a commodity or a thing and thereby can be bought or sold.

It is the thinking mind that conceives of a soul.

The thinking mind implies the I.

And, the I is not eternal, though it is human desire to believe that the soul is indivisible from the I.

Thus, in terms of eternity, it does not exist. It is not a commodity and cannot be bought or sold.

The Christians belief of selling the soul holds no validity.

741

Man perceives the selling of the soul as the most horrid of all things. This concept and process is completely programmed into one by society though the practice is based in desire, superstition, and psychic energy control.

Whether or not the person receives their desired goal or gift is unimportant. They, by their own mind, damn themselves to psychic hell forever.

742

When there is no desire, there is nothing to sell your soul for.

743

Siddhartha Guatama, the Buddha said to live the
middle path, live in moderation.

But, he and his avid devotees did not.

His path was completely to one side, the side of
asceticism. Did he not see his own illusion?

744

The Buddha believed that life was a means to
something else, namely, a higher incarnation.

He was wrong.
Life is a means to nothing.
It is perfect in its own moment, for its own sake.

745

It is a foolish concept to believe, as the Buddha did,
that after becoming disheartened with life and
seeing things alien and distasteful to you that if you
sat down in one spot, the truth would come to you.

The truth is already there in the no truth, in the
perfection of the distasteful and it is only the
thinking mind that believes that this is not so.

746

The thinking mind led the Buddha to shun the material world. The thinking mind led the Buddha to sit under the bodhi tree. The thinking mind led the Buddha to believe that there is temptation. The thinking mind led the Buddha to believe that he "knew." The thinking mind led the Buddha to desire to go out and become the teacher to those he believed knew less than himself.

747

The Buddha, after becoming frustrated with the world, sat down under the bodhi tree, until he realized the cause of suffering is desire. Once he arrived at this, he still remained in his physical body that he had to feed, give water, and keep up.

He failed to see his own folly. Keeping the body alive is the strongest natural desire and this is where all problems of the world begin.

748

The Buddha spoke of total equality. Was the Buddha the same as his disciples? No, they revered him, took care of him, worshiped him.

749

The Buddha, when asked, said he was only a man. It is his disciples that have made him more than a man.

750

What did the Buddha prove?

He taught that desire was the cause of suffering, but what led him to this conclusion was a desire, and now all of his disciples have made the same mistake and desire to be just like him. They have set up a religion full of dogma, fanaticism, and necessary techniques in an attempt to achieve what they believe is Buddhahood.

The Buddha failed. All he left was another religion full of desire.

751

The Buddha wanted to have followers or else there would not have been followers. The same is true with Jesus, Mohammed, and all other teachers.

752

All the great religious leaders and knowers were only human, and no matter how much their followers try to say or make up about them; waiting in other worlds, watching, judging, and so on, they are only lying to themselves. For these teachers were human, and as human, they died. Sad, but true.

753

The founders of Islam were very wise. They proclaimed, that if one fights in a holy war and dies, they will go to the greatest heaven. This gives its followers a reason to fight with all of their power, holding nothing back, believing it is a passage to God's kingdom.

Is a holy war simply not a particular group's point of view?

754

All religions are inherently bad. They breed dependency, ritual, and an invalid morality.

755

Is there a God, or do you just desire there to be a God?

756

Does your belief in God or your lack of belief in God change the fact that there is or is not a God?
757

Man wants to believe in something.

758

Belief systems are not worth believing in.

759

People all believe in the promise of heaven,
until they feel that they deserve hell.

Then they all say, "I don't believe in that."

760

Man is human.

Thus, imagines all things in human form,

       including God.

761

People do not just simply believe in something.

Though the mindless may state that this is so.

Belief is a choice, influenced by fear or desire.

762

The greatest mistake of religion was to encourage
procreation and claim that God validated it. For this
is the root problem of today's food shortages and
poverty.

763

In earlier times of human evolution, more people were considered to be spiritual. This is due to the fact that superstition was much stronger, there was less understanding, and people needed something to hold on to.

Now, people have seen that science has proven many of the old superstitions wrong. Thus, doubt the spiritual way and choose to pursue the more scientific explanation of life.

Spiritual or superstition, it is a fine line.

764

In the time of Lao Tsu, perhaps one in ten were followers of the Tao. Now, it is more like one in ten thousand, but still that one person makes the difference in this world.

765

Superstition is for important people.

Religion is superstition.

766

Religious people are not conscious people.

Religious people are superstitious people.

767

For a man to be a true mystic, he must first master
the dark side, not simply understand it, but conquer
it.

Knowing the light is easy, but the dark side tempts
and holds one.

Understanding the good and the bad. All is known.

768

To hide from the dark forces, one is controlled by
the dark forces.

769

There are many truths that are told, but most
teachers borrow knowledge to relay wisdom.

Few have truly experienced what they teach.

770

The main problem with being a teacher of anything
is getting caught up with the fact that you are a
teacher.

771

How can you know when one has experienced what
they teach?

772

Many spiritual teachers claim that they were almost enlightened in their past life, but came back to this physical existence to finish it up.

Truth or business?

773

Why should one believe a teacher who speaks of the infinite? What proof do they have?

774

If someone feels that they know the truth, are enlightened, and wish to teach what they know to others, they are saying, "I know something, you do not."

How does their ego come into play in this?

775

If one wishes to be a teacher, they must keep the student under the illusion that they know much more than them.

776

A teacher gives out a little knowledge at a time, making the learning processes appear more difficult than it actually is. The student believes that there is much more to learn.

777

One who states, "Do not follow me, instead become like me." sets the stage for discipleship. What the are actually saying is, "I have something that you do not."

778

Disciple = puppet.

779

Ego breeds the teacher, not truth.

The minute one feels that they know more than another or feels that they have something to teach, truth is lost and ego is in play.

Jesus, Buddha, Mohammed,

all were egomaniacs.

780

The problem with being in a system where there is a supreme leader is that one may fall from grace with them, due to actions or personality conflicts.

781

If a mystic can find work as a teacher of mysticism, there is not much of a problem. But, if they cannot, what doe the mystic do?

782

Jesus, Buddha, Mohammed, and all spiritual
teachers are devils.

Why? Because they spread the lie that there is
something else, some other place to be, some other
world or life to wait for. Thus, people do not take
full advantage of their short time of life here on
earth.

783

Spiritual teachers and groups always make up little
slogans like: truth is one, the paths to it are many,
the spiritual sun rose in the east but will set in the
west, and so on. These are to give the group
definition and segregation, but it is actually just
mental masturbation. One should not waste their
time with slogans and not separate themselves from
others, with the inner group knowledge that they
think they have.

784

Spiritual leaders use words and sayings that are only
known to the inner circle of a group.

Mention it to an outsider, they will not understand.

785

Words are coined to make a system seem deeper
than it is.

786

A spiritual teacher gives names and titles to separate
who they believe is the lower and the higher.

787

If a teacher believes that there is a lower and higher,
they are not a true teacher.

All humans are equal, in consciousness and
understanding.

It is the unenlightened who believe that
consciousness is something that you get or
something that you are or are not.

788

Enlightenment is if you are.

789

There are no saints.

A man who proclaims himself one is an egotist.

A group who calls somebody one is being fooled.

790

If one is to lay down a system of spiritual teachings,
they should have it fully mapped out beforehand
and not change course midstream.

791

Just because one is a spiritual teacher does not make them always right.

792

Being a spiritual teacher is the most conscious way of soaking up love and affection.

793

A person receives some sort of initiation or spiritual insight and the mindless flock to them, calling them holy and feeling that individual is so much higher than themselves and should be revered.

Who is the fool, the followers or the person deceiving them self that they know more than anyone else?

794

A spiritual teacher is more bound by ego than any other person alive.

795

Sannyas, monkhood, renunciation.

> The ultimate hype, becoming nothing
> is becoming something.

796

The Zen monk pours tea into a man's cup, over filling it and letting the tea continue to pour, to demonstrate that the man is like the tea cup, too full.

The Zen monk then is demonstrating as well that he also is too full and has superiority over the other man.

Where do the too full teacups stop?

797

In teaching spirituality, one does not have to teach meditation and prayer. One must discuss illusion-lifting methods and help others to see through to the heart of common everyday experiences.

798

All the people who talk of spiritual matters are simply placing themselves above others. It is completely egotistical, that they have something to give, and you have something to learn. It is the greatest con, the biggest pick-up line.

If a person who speaks of spirituality says something, "is," don't believe it; believe the opposite. The worldly are much more holy than a spiritual teacher.

799

What is the reason a person teaches spirituality?

800

The biggest problem on the spiritual path is forgetting spiritual vision.

Once you know too much, it is easy to forget.

801

It is easy for one to say that in a past life they were this person or that. For there is no way to prove it.

802

If you have not experienced it in this life, you have not experienced it.

803

The mystic has the very bad habit of coming to the conclusion that they know more, understand more, have seen more, and are therefore better than the average person.

804

Spirituality gives one reasons and excuses for everything.

805

Spirituality is not for someone who doesn't have time.

806

Do you wish to be spiritual for yourself, for your
own realization and understanding, or do you wish
to be spiritual to benefit others?

807

Is being spiritual being selfish?

808

The yogi says, "Silence the thinking mind."

But, silence is only a thought.

809

You cannot speak to some one about mysticism;

they will not hear you.

They either already are it or they will never be it.

810

Few understand mysticism.

This is what makes it mystical.

811

There are many pretend mystics.

812

Zen training, such as walking three steps, stopping and bowing is to teach one, who does not yet realize it, the ridiculousness and illusion of life. Many practitioners find purpose and ego gratification in this, however and thus, never realize the purpose of the exercise.

813

If this world is real or unreal is a philosophic argument.

814

In spirituality, there is no freedom.

Spirituality breeds conscience. Conscience breeds guilt. Guilt leads to lack of freedom.

815

Mysticism is not what you say. Mysticism is what you live.

816

Can you see another person's visions?

817

Practical intelligence is not spiritual wisdom, but spiritual wisdom does not pay the bills.

818

The conflict of spirituality and the world.

A person who has progressed along the spiritual path for a time will begin to see that all is perfect; that everything has a reason.

The one problem with seeing all as perfect is that one begins to take no action, and there is no motivation to change undesirable circumstances.

819

Do you realize the perfection of the universe?

820

The average person believes that one is only enlightened when they lead a very austere life, a monk in a cave or a priest in a temple. It is not believed that a person who lives in the world can be or is enlightened. What a foolish concept.

821

Enlightenment is where you find it.

822

Does standing on one leg for a year or not speaking make you a saint?

823

Doing physical things does not make one a saint.

824

Even the enlightened man must eat, drink, sleep,
and breathe.

825

What does an enlightened person do to support
himself?

826

The businessman makes his living from speaking to
God. The enlightened man does not.

827

A man who throws away hi morals is a sinner. A
man who has no morals is a saint.

828
When an artist sells their art, they become only a
businessman.

When an enlightened man teaches their knowledge,
they become only a businessman.

829

An enlightened man is just a man.

830

What does being enlightened prove?

831

Does enlightenment make one a superior person?

832

What is enlightenment?

833

Enlightenment is not a thing.

834

Enlightenment is described differently by each person who claims that they have obtained it.

Are all enlightenments equal?

835

How many just read a book on spiritual experiences and convince themselves that they have had one?

836

People expect something to happen from meditation and spiritual practices. When it does occur, they say, "Finally."

An experience is not enlightenment.

Truth only exists when nothing is happening.

837

One has to lose or forget language before they can understand the cosmic.

838

Nirvana cannot be put into words.

839

Words have definitions with mental pictures and thoughts connected to them.

This is why they block cosmic understanding.

840

To use words such as mantras to obtain cosmic freedom will not work and simply hypnotizes the mind. It only leads to a definition of a word, not enlightenment.

841

Be so free that you need nothing in your hands and have nothing in your head.

842

From meaning, one can never find no meaning.

No meaning is what is sought in enlightenment.

843

Colorful experiences are not enlightenment. They
are just experiences.

If they were, then every person ever to take a drug
would be enlightened.

844

The reason spiritual experiences are not
enlightenment is that they are temporal.

Enlightenment is forever, and there is no need for
temporal experiences.

845

Peak experiences are like taking mind-altering
drugs.

They accelerate the consciousness for a time, but
they are not permanent.

846

If one moves into a place of continual peak
experience, then it becomes commonplace.

From there, it must become deeper and accelerated
to achieve the same high, the same syndrome of any
drug addict on the street needing more and more.

847

It is believed in mysticism that all are enlightened.
They just do not realize that they are.

Most people of this world do not care about
enlightenment, and the few who do desire
realization, are caught in the illusion that they do
not yet already possess it.

So, to those who do not care, it never enters their
mind. Thus, it means nothing. To those who feel it
is far away, it will forever be out of reach. Thus,
never known, it can never be understood.

All are not enlightened.

848

The reason people do not understand that they are
already enlightened is because they have a
preconceived notion of what enlightenment is
supposed to be.

This definition that enlightenment is something
difficult and far away has been passed down by
false teachers since time began.

Thus, people do not believe that they have the
ability to reach such a high place.

849

There is this well received Buddhist text. The author stated, in the introduction, that he was saddened at the lack of progress that he had made.

The only sad thing is that he never realized the illusion that there is no progress to make and being just where you are is the perfect place to be.

850

Spiritual growth and enlightenment is not a race.

851

Spiritual awakening comes in strange forms.

852

A disciple can never obtain enlightenment.

853

Enlightenment is not money. It does not provide financial security.

854

Enlightenment is easy.

855

Life is an addiction.

All people are addicts of one kind of another.

856

All are bound by their beliefs.

857

It is impossible to find balance in one's life.

Either one does everything or does nothing.

If one does everything, much is left undone. If one does nothing, then nothing is accomplished. Thus, balance is impossible. Those who claim to have it are lying to themselves and others.

858

There are many energies in the world, other than visible.

People unconsciously invoke them, by continually speaking or thinking of them.

People should not be so unconscious of what they think, feel, or say for the outcome may be undesirable.

859

Fulfillment of desire equals zero.

For with the fulfillment of one desire, a new desire is born.

860

Everyone should have a self-destruct button.

      Death before dishonor.

861

Karma yoga or selfless service promises rewards in this and the next life. But, these promises always seem to be made by the one who is desirous of the free service.

862

Who are you doing selfless service for, yourself or another?

863

One may gain strength from another's weakness. One may gain courage from another's fear. One may gain insight from another's stupidity.

864

A high IQ or fame does not make one great.

865

Exercising, sports, going to the health spas, people do these activities for health, prolonged life, good looks, and so on. Yet, if they were required to do these same tasks as a form of manual labor, they would all become quite angered.

866

To the best of one's ability not only implies desire,
but physical, psychological, emotional strength, and
education as well.

867

The purpose of all financial ventures is to isolate a
specific item. Define a given market for it, then
release it, and charge the highest price that will be
accepted.

It is not necessarily conscious, but it is reality.

868

What is done from a pure space requires no
payment.

869

It is interesting how people take pride in themselves
when they accomplish something devious over
another person.

For example, when one gets too much change back,
when they beat someone to a parking space, when
they steal something, or get something free.

In other words, man takes pride in getting away
with things. It is sad that society has bred people so
small minded that there is pleasure gained in these
areas.

870

If the average person states that something is not right, it is felt that they are simply complaining.

If a renowned person claims something is not right, all believe that an important statement is being made.

871

Simply because something is felt to be wrong, does not mean that it is wrong.

872

There is no such thing as right or wrong.

873

Right or wrong is only fed by emotion.

874

There is no such thing as right and wrong, there is only the acceptance or the non-acceptance of what is taking place.

875

Availability is the only defining factor.

876

Choices are governed by availability.

877

Circumstances lead one to life's choices.

878

Circumstances dominate life.

879

All that is taught is not necessarily the truth.

880

Philosophy is complex.
Religion is complex.
Magic is complex.
Psychic realms are complex.

       Truth is simple.

To obtain truth's simplicity, throw away the rest.

881

When one states that they wish to help someone,
words are simply not enough.

One must put thoughts into action and do
something.

882

Listen to your inner feelings.

       If you live right, they will be right.

883

The world is dominated by the egotist.

Teachers believe that they have something to teach.
Politicians think that they have someone to lead.
Lovers think that they have something to get.
Losers thing that they have nothing to give, get or
teach. All are forms of ego. There is no one in the
world that is not dominated by it.

884

A lot of people claim to know the key to life.

Talk is cheap.

885

The fact is, around every bend, you never know
where the next illusion may lie.

886

Spiritualists and naturalists often speak of their
desire to return to the freedom of being as a bird or
an animal.

This may be a nice poetic idea, but man is the
dominant creature on this planet, and if one were to
return to that lower evolutionary position, it would
be doubtful that they would enjoy it.

Animals need to seek out shelter and food as well.

887

The best vengeance is no vengeance at all.

For then the opponent is not given the glory of our honoring their previous victory.

888

How many things in this world have been meant to be done?

889

What would this world be like if all the things that were meant to be done were actually accomplished?

890

Trying is a waste of time.

       Either do it or do not do it.

891

There is no glare in a world that has nothing to reflect.

892

Theft, sex, violence, parenthood are all momentary highs that the now confused world is seeking to fulfill momentary power desires.

893

Why do people succeed?

They desire power.

894

It is difficult to manipulate a cynic.

895

When you have limited space, you do limited
things.

896

The problem with going out on a limb is that you
have to come back in or fall.

897

The news is so temporary.

898

The way one chooses to live life is defined by their
own perceptions.

One person buys expensive things and looks down
on those who do not.

Another buys bargain items and cannot understand
why others choose to spend so much.

899

"I did not mean it that way."

Words, how they are meant and how they are said.

How ridiculous.

900

People aspire to have the qualities they admire.
Yet, they wish those who do have them would come
down to their level.

901

Thoughts are in the form of words.

As long as the thoughts are in the form of words,
they hold no truth.

902

You didn't know it then because you weren't ready
to know it then.

903

Left alone, life will handle itself.

904

Thinking is not knowing.

905

Knowledge may be deep but a body is just a body, a mind is just a mind.

906

Great is not necessarily good.

      Great is only great.

907

The more you can do, the more complicated life becomes.

908

Doubt is what ultimately leads to truth.

909

A little doubt is healthy.

910

Where is the certainty?

The certainty is in belief.

911

Blessed are the sinners, for they are the ones with the experience to know what they are talking about.

912

If one stays long enough, they too will pass through that time period.

913

There simply are no excuses.

914

Have you ever . . .

915

Simply because someone believes that they need something or someone does not necessarily make it true.

916

Interaction and inner-reflection do not mix.

917

Those who are involved never die.

918

A dream based in lies turns into a nightmare.

919

Nothing.

The only thing that is perfect within itself.

920

Some people have the ability to be involved in a discussion that is not in their field of expertise and yet, still appear to know what they are talking about. These people may be deemed wise simply due to this ability, but in fact it is completely the contrary. For in doing this, they show that they have presupposed concepts and ideas based on previously gained unrelated knowledge. Therefore, they rob themselves of gaining new wisdom.

921

If it just doesn't matter, you can walk away.

922

You are either created by the world or you create the world.

If you are created by it, there are mistakes, guilt, and regrets.

If you create it, there is control, dynamics, and definition.

923

There is always a war somewhere.

924

War is where you make it.

925

Mostly, people speak a lot about their ideas or concepts, and no one really knows anything about what is actually going on.

926

We have all been someplace.

If a person can accept where another has been, then the two can be together.

927

Whether it is your own fault or not, it does not mean that it can't hurt you, too.

928

Are you addicted to your medicine?

929

Controlling the breath grounds one.

The breath is physical. Thus, concentrating on it is grounding.

930

Why do you do things that are bad for your body?

931

Art is not an object.

It is how one views things.

932

The purpose of a photograph is to view the whole
scene, and then isolate a specific area of it. Thus,
making it art.

933

Interpretation of art and literature is simply the
speculation of fools.

934

Creativity by its very nature proves to be
unspiritual.

Spirituality equals simplicity. Creativity, on the
other hand, requires objects such as instruments,
brushes, paper, and so on. It is not free of
interaction with material objects. Thus, not
spiritual.

935

All that art can be is the artist's perception.

936

What makes an artist an artist is that they do it; the
rest of the world does not.

937

To be an artist, you must make everything you do,
every thought you think art.

938

What are movies and television? Visual literature.

939

If you wish the world to appreciate art, you must
bring art into every place that you go, your clothing,
your hair, your words, and your actions.

940

Authors who write about themselves,

      painters who paint of themselves,

      photographers who picture themselves

         wish to be cast to eternity.

941

How much of life do you really take the time to
see?

942

Refinement is in the eye of the beholder. The rest
see it as just a passing mass in the movement of life.

943

If you choose to be sophisticated, you separate
yourself from the common man.

944

If you make moves and take actions that are not
done fully consciously, someone, maybe you, will
get hurt.

945

Change may happen in a moment,

but it is the test of time that proves its validity.

946

We need to push the limits of whatever situation we
find ourselves in.

947

If you wish to be nothing,

then you have already succeeded.

948

Dreams never die,

they just become spirits.

949

In this world there are three types of people.

      1. People who are trying to get somewhere

      2. People who are somewhere.

      3. People who were somewhere and
          continually reminisce of it.

950

Simplicity is obviously the answer, not necessarily the answer.

951

You can't take anything with you, but you can leave a lot behind.

952

Life is an individual perception.

953

There are no players in this world; there are only winners and losers.

954

It is unfortunate, but the world is just another place.

955

Mostly, it is just a long way to nowhere.

956

What is all progress? Simply ideas that work.

957

The majority of opinion(s) are based in ego.

958

Insanity is a fine art.

959

People readily buy the false illusion that one person's holiness surpasses their own simply because of external images. The same is true with intelligence, finances, power, and so on.

Play the game well, and others will believe the same of you.

960

There is always one card left to play.

961

Age gives things value.

It does not necessarily give things worth.

962

Is any life fulfilled?

963

Life, it is all just amusing.

964

If you have to call yourself something: a doctor, a mystic, an artist, a fool; then you are nothing.

What you are should be obvious with out titles or clothing.

965

Maturity is just an individual definition.

966

If you want to do something, do it.

Don't make excuses:
       physical,
       psychological,
       or spiritual
       for not doing it.

967

There are very strong energy vibrations in the office of a psychologist, due to all the negative emotions encountered there.

968

A person who is a psychologist should first learn to be a psychic-logist, for then they will not be swayed, moved, or destroyed by the unseen forces of the ethereal realms.

969

In psychoanalysis, the patient may make an erroneous self-statement based on anger, fear, or stress. The psychologist then may put more emphasis on it than actually should be, leaving the person with a falsely guided self-description.

970

The psychological technique is to dig deeply into a person to find out the reason that they may be troubled, but in doing this, they may reveal things to the individual that they are not yet ready to confront. Thus, doing more harm than good.

971

A psychologist or psychiatrist is just a person. They have emotions, feelings, and desires, too.

972

When a person reaches a certain time in their life, they begin to know who and what they are. But, these understandings are based in ego, desires, and the programmed input of the surrounding environment, not by enlightenment or deep self-reflection.

973

People on the whole have the tendency to enter into
a space of believing something about themselves,
and they never choose to change.

974

The things one is taught in their childhood stays
with them.

> If it is positive, very good.

> If it is negative, it takes much undoing.

975

It is you who decides to think or feel anything.

How many people really believe that?
How many prefer to choose to blame others?

976

You create your own anger.

977

It is you who decides whether or not to become
angry. Do not blame situations or other people.

978

If you are not controlling you, who is controlling
you?

979

A psychological or spiritual book or tape that makes
you feel good for a time is just the same as a drug;
the feeling is fleeting.

980

A peak experience is just a feeling, and feelings
come and go.

981

If you want to be self actualized, just don't care
about anything. It is as simple as that.

982

Call it personality, destiny, or programming, some
people, no matter how much or how often they are
knocked down will get back up and make the best
of it.

983

How many people who speak of not letting yourself
be a victim have every been a victim,

          physically, psychologically, or otherwise?

984

Being a victim is your choice.

It is you who chooses to feel a certain way about
any life experience.

985

Virtually every one has felt a certain amount of
psychological instability in their life, either self
induced or created externally.

Let it go and it will not haunt you.

986

Everything a person does, every choice that they
make is based in psychological and environmental
influences, accompanied by a little bit of inborn
personality.

987

Life = death.

988

No one wants to die, not even the suicidal, for life is
all that we know. One just wishes life to be
different and thereby, desires an alternative.

Death, being the only option.

989

One dies within their own vision.

990

Life is a progressive dis-ease. We are all going to
die.

991

There are too many people who are dying and desiring to live. And, too many people living and wishing to die. And, the rest, they simply pass from birth to death, and do not even notice it.

992

Pleasure and pain is a physical principal.

Therefore, it cannot exist after death.

993

Death is just meeting a new stranger.

994

Life is like being asleep and in a dream.

When you die, you wake up and the dream is over.

995

Death is just like moving to a new neighborhood.

996

Suicide is based in unfulfilled desires.

997

The reasons people kill themselves is that they are not getting their own way.

998

When you become death, death cannot become you.

999

Why is the person who wishes to die always convinced that it is not their fault that they feel that way?

1000

There are more important things to occupy your mind with than thoughts of death.

1001

Worldly man must take care of himself.

Spiritual man sees all as being taken care of.

1002

It is far easier for one to focus on the bad and negative experiences that they have had in this life because then one can feel sorry for them self and gain a warped sense of self fulfillment and a negatively based feeling of reward, blaming others. It is far more productive however, to remember the good and positive times. They being brought into focus will bring about similar positive experiences, instead of further negative ones.

1003

The mind finds false contentment in feeling sorry
for itself.

1004

When you don't know who is at fault for life not
being the way that you want it to be, you try to find
someone to blame.

The truth is you are the one who let it become a
specific way, not another person or a situation.

1005

If you simply do not care which direction life takes
and you have no desire or care what you end up
doing, the mind is free and life is lived happily.

1006

Set yourself free.

1007

People generally have children for all the wrong
reasons. They wish to have a pet or a puppet, not
thinking and feeling person.

1008

Parents raise children completely wrong. They use
pain, guilt, and threats as a means of obtaining their
own desired results from the child.

1009

If a person is going to have a child, they must be psychologically strong enough to allow the child to be what ever it wants to be, and think what ever it chooses.

1010

Why do you wish to have a child?

Is the answer based in your own desire?

Then, you cannot be a good parent.

1011

You are not too old to get young yet.

1012

If you are not happy, you must be willing to change you own self-image.

If you are not willing to change your own self-image, you must find happiness in what you find now is unhappy.

1013

Conflict is conflicting.

1014

The way knowledge grows is that an individual or a group collects as much information as is available on a specific subject, assimilates it, removing all of the inconsistency and unnecessary wording, leaving only what is necessary. Thus, it becomes a complete system from which the individuals it is passed on to can easily understand, and move forward with their own insights and observations.

1015

Yes, you may have seen it before, but what if you never were to see it again?

1016

Life is measured by the amount of memories and experiences that one has had, be they good or bad.

1017

The majority of people bind them self physically, emotionally, spiritually as they get older, by what they think that they know.

1018

The world weights us down by what we are suppose to do, how we are suppose to feel, what we are suppose to like or dislike, and so on.

There is so little room for differentiation.

1019

Criticism does not help anything or anybody.

1020

It is a lot harder to pick up the pieces than to never
have them broken in the first place.

1021

All things are within their own range.

1022

Even in the down times, there are up times.

1023

There are two truths:
Perceived truth, which varies according to what a
person believes and absolute truth, which is not
influenced by individual perceptions.

1024

Absolute truth.

Many speak of it; many claim that they know it.
Some that speak of this knowledge have followers
who believe that they do possess it; some do not.

Why then is the absolute truth of each of these
people different?
Should the absolute truth of everyone not be the
same?

1025

If you have to debate whether or not something is truthful, then it is a lie.

1026

Selective truth is not truth.

1027

Life is just an experience and there is no absolute truth or reason.

1028

The truth...
> most of this world's opinions are based on people's lies.

1029

Reality is a funny thing. If someone tells you something and you believe it to be true, then it is true. What if they lied? What if they spoke with knowledge that they did not have? Would it still then be true? Truth is completely speculative and changes with the understanding of each individual person. Thus, there is no such thing as absolute truth. In fact, even momentary truth is in flux and completely dominated by the understanding and beliefs of the individual.

1030

Logic is a point of view.

1031

We all have a different meaning of and for life.

1032

Why me God?

"Because you play."

1033

Doing things a little at a time requires the same amount of time and energy as letting things build up and doing them all at once.

1034

Hurt feelings are based in the control or the lack of control of a given situation.

Having it happen the way one wants, one is happy.

If a situation is not going the way one wants, one is tolerant at best.

Therefore, feeling happy or sad is all based in control or the lack thereof.

1035

If your eyes are closed, there is no confusion, only
darkness.

1036

Knowing without knowing, the key to all illusion.

1037

Do you ever contemplate how much of the
knowledge that you have and the things that you do
is suggested or inspired by others?

1038

The outcome of a person is obviously effected by
outside influences.

1039

You may always think things are going to change
and get better, but until you decide to make them
change and make them get better, nothing will
occur.

1040

If dreams are supposed journeys into the astral
realms, why then do two or more people not have
the same dream experience?

Why then, if one is dreaming about someone else,
does not the other person have the same dream?

1041

The psychic realms may exist.

But, if so, they are filled with as much illusion as this physical realm.

1042

Simply because one has a psychic experience related to another person does not mean that it effects that other person.

1043

If one desires to see and feel other energies, one opens them self up to forces that they may not have the ability to control

1044

The most powerful magician is one with no doubt.

1045

In black or satanic rituals, they reverse white, traditional, or natural symbolism and techniques in an attempt to invoke the power of the opposite.

Nature has a pattern, it will never be altered and though these energies may be momentarily reversed, the patterns will return to their natural course. That is just the way of the universe.

1046

Simply by having the knowledge of occult defense,
one is protected because not only psychologically is
one stronger, but occult forces realize the
individual's ability.

1047

One of the best forms of psychic self-defense is to
consciously not let the thoughts of a person enter
your mind.

1048

No thought,
no visual picture,
no ability to have psychic contact.

1049

For one to have any type of psychic contact with a
person, the thought of that person must first be
present.

1050

A simple thought of a person is a form of psychic
contact.

1051

Public figures are continually in the position of
being bombarded by psychic energy influences.

1052

To enter into the psychic/astral realm, one must first lose all ideas and concepts of what they think that it is.

1053

What is the purpose of entering into the psychic/astral realm?

Some say to gain higher knowledge or to grow spiritually. These are things, however, that are linked to the physical form, and the concept of I.

When one realizes that I is not permanent, then one no longer sets out to obtain these worthless advancements.

1054

Chasing the psychic is like desiring money. One may have the best intentions, but the chase will bind one, and they will never be free.

1055

Being totally in the now, one loses all foundation, all reference, all time frame. It is only when you are not in the now that you can say that you were in the now. And, by being completely in the now, life passes just the same, with the disadvantage of no memory to recall and rekindle enjoyable feelings.

1056

Before you judge a person, you should attempt to understand their emotional and psychological condition.

1057

Even if they are not there for you, be there for them.

1058

There is always something more to do and to get.

1059

Wait until it happens.

1060

Is everyone in Heaven beautiful?

1061

Have you ever watched a drink disappear as it is sliding down your throat?

1062

How many single grains of rice are lost while cleaning it or once you are full?

How quickly would those single grains of discarded rice fill an empty bowl?

1063

Vegetarians who begin to eat meat always find a
good excuse for why they did so.

1064

Why is it said, "Return to being as little children,"
or "See the world through the eyes of a child?"

Children's decisions, thoughts, and desires are
based purely on the emotions of the moment. Their
opinions are formed around momentary sensory
gratification. Why is it good to be like that?

1065

Children, adolescents, and most adults are
motivated by desire, power, control, and momentary
gratification.

Their opinions mean nothing.

1066

People settle into their own patterns and never take
the time to look at life. They do not realize that one
makes up their own mind and creates their own fate
and destiny.

People remain poor, angry, even cause their own
fatal illness because they either believe that they
have no control or are afraid to take control over
life's situations.

Are you trapped in your own life's patterns?

1067

Are you wise enough to see the impermanence of love?

1068

What is love?

1069

Does love exist, or is it simply attraction and infatuation that moves on to attachment?

1070

Those who philosophies about love are not in love.

1071

A broken heart is like a little girl who has her animal crackers eaten by her pet dog. She lays on the floor and cries until she is given new ones.

1072

If problems exist within a relationship, whether they be self inflicted or simply come into being by outside influences, there can be little room for love.

Attachment, possessiveness, "Yes."

But, love, "No."

1073

It is easy to convince one's own self to leave a relationship.

It is much harder to convince one's own self to stay.

1074

Life and relationships are based in concentric circles, focusing around a central point.

There is a focal point.

Then there is the closest circle.

Then the circles that go out from there.

1075

The reason people often times have psychological problems post the breakup of a long-term relationship is that the psychic bond that was developed is broken.

Then the individual has no one's support or energy to rely on.

The only buffer for this is if a person goes directly from one relationship to the next.

1076

Going directly from one relationship to the next shows disrespect for the previous partner.

1077

Intimacy takes a long time to develop.

The reason a person often times leaves a new relationship, returning to an old one is because they long for the intimacy that has not yet had the chance to grow.

1078

To break the intimacy of being a couple by cheating on your partner proves nothing.

1079

How would you feel if your mate was doing the same thing that you are doing?

1080

People always say prior to their marriage,

"We won't end up like them."

It is unfortunate, but in almost all cases, that is exactly what happens.

1081

The person who can love you the most is simply the person who is the most addicted to you.

1083

One does not wish to die for a person or thing
because of love.

One wishes to die due to their attachment to that
person or thing and the falsely programmed belief
that love is proved that way.

1084

Love by its definition cannot last.

Love is an emotion. Emotions by their very nature
come, go, and change.

Therefore, love is a temporal emotion,

a temporary thing.

1085

Love is more than the feeling in your heart. Love
requires positive conscious action, directed towards
a common goal.

1086

Love, is a choice that you make.

1087

Orgasm. So much of the world's happiness, pain,
longing, and fantasies are based upon it.

1088

People who do not have sex wear the amount of
times that they have been abstinence around their
neck like a trophy.

Those who have a lot of sex wear the amount of
conquests around their neck like a trophy.

Those who have had no sex, but wish they had are
silent.

Where does the purity lie?

1089

Why do certain spiritualists believe sex is wrong?

If two people are both interested, there is nothing
wrong with it at all, and it can lead one to many
realizations.

1090

Without attempting sex,

>   without mastering sex,

>   one cannot criticize sex.

1091

What does sex fulfill?

1092

If you are dominated and controlled by the desire
for sex, how can you ever expect to have control
over the much more important aspects of life?

1093

A man is at his most vulnerable point when he is
making love to a woman.

1094

The majority of people desire sex.

Thus, they seek enlightenment.

Why is sex desired?

For the blissful feeling obtained in orgasm that is
not dissimilar to the sensation of higher spiritual
experience.

1095

Some compare the experience of orgasm to that of
samadhi.

    Orgasm is felt in the mind.

    Samadhi is felt in the mind.

1096

Both orgasm and samadhi are experienced in the mind.

Both have physical methods that are developed to bring them about.

Thus, both orgasm and samadhi are based in physical, not spiritual activities.

The difference is, the average person seeks only orgasm while the spiritual person, whether it be a physical activity or not, seeks only enlightenment.

1097

The body and mind lead one to the feeling of orgasm.

The mind trains the experiences and heightens the intensity.

The body and mind lead one to the feeling of samadhi.

The mind trains the experience and heightens the intensity.

1098

The mind has been programmed with the expected results of both orgasm and samadhi.

Neither can be fully understood until they are experienced.

1099

It is stated by some that orgasm is a chemical reaction in the brain. Is samadhi then, the developed ability to release that same chemical in the brain consciously, not dissimilar to that of a runner who by jogging, unknowingly releases a drug like substance in the brain, which then gives a euphoric feeling?

1100

Is orgasm samadhi?

1101

Orgasm is an interesting phenomenon.

You have to do a certain activity to obtain a certain type of result.

1102

There are two people inside all of us: the physical and the spiritual. And, no matter how much we try to hide from either aspect, they both affect us.

1103

If you speak of being happy, you become happy.

1104

After something is destroyed, it doesn't matter if you believed in it or not.

1105

You cannot know a person's true nature until they are pushed over the edge.

1106

If you want your realizations to remain timeless, make them in areas that no one can prove or disprove.

1107

No matter how wrong a person may be, they still believe that they are right.

1108

Words lie.

1109

If you give a person, in any relationship, the opportunity to realize that they can live with out you, you will never have the same control over them again.

1110

People from oppressed and impoverished lands need to believe in life after death and another chance.

This is their method of hope and survival.

1111

Just because a belief serves a purpose does not
make it a valid belief.

1112

Mistakes are just a point of view.

1113

There is no art in compliancy.

1114

Morality does not bring happiness.

It simply makes one numb.

1115

The fool tries to seek meaning in the words of
others.

1116

One should not make blanket statements,
judgments, or observations.

For each individual situation is influenced by so
many variables.

1117

Sometimes life is just not all that understandable.

1118

Experience is what you make of it.

1119

What you don't do, you don't have to un-do.

1120

If your internal life is in disrepair, you seek to go out.

If your external life is in disrepair,

      you seek to stay in.

1121

Though their points of view may be different and their answer may one day be proven, right or wrong, a great thinker will forever be known as a great thinker.

1122

Smoking, drinking, or taking drugs proves that an individual has begun to believe the illusion that there is something more to life than this here and now reality.

1123

The only benefit of alcohol or drugs is that it gives one a moment of not caring.

1124

If under the influence of alcohol or drugs, you are not yourself, then who are you?

1125

If drugs are so bad, why do they make you feel so good?

1126

The taking of drugs and alcohol does not make you holy.

The not taking of drugs and alcohol does not make you holy.

1127

It is easy to find a way to break something.

 It is very difficult to find a way to fix it.

1128

Once something is broken, it can never really be fixed.

1129

If you wish to remain sane and happy,

       you must make the mundane holy.

1130

Is meeting a person at a ballet anymore auspicious
than meeting them at a massage parlor?

1131

Where do thoughts come from?

1132

Where did the first thought come from?

1133

If you live your life on a grandiose scale, the simple
things have so little value.

1134

When your world is very small,

        small things will make you happy.

1135

You can never really understand another person.
1136

The mind loves to find things to think about.

1137

If you choose to be different, society will shut you
out.

1138

Because(s) equal zero.

1139

If you want to be out of the mainstream, don't
expect life to be easy.

1140

We base our opinion of a person on what they say.
But how much of what they say is true and how
much of it is simply made up for the benefit of the
person they are speaking with?

1141

In Heaven, what do you dream of?

1142

Just because someone says that they will die for you
does not mean that they would die for you.

1143

The more that you do, the more that is left undone.

1144

It is not important what a person does with their
personal life.

What is important is whether a person helps others
to be more conscious.

1145

If they give you an ultimatum, they are not true of heart.

1146

Once is an accident. Twice, you are making a habit of it.

1147

Life is just short stories making up a book.

1148

When someone has something to gain, they are always a nice person.

1149

You can only win when you play to win.

1150

What is so perfect about perfection?
1151

It is not hard to be positive.

1152

Just because a person is old and smiles a lot does not mean that they were a good person in younger years.

1153

A watch judges time only by how accurately you set it.

1154

When the present is empty, people think of revivals.

1155

If one allows disorganization, at some point the disorganization will take control.

1156

The only problem with life is that there is no operating manual.

1157

People attempt to find reasons for causation, be it astrology, destiny, karma, or fate. But, is there any reason for causation?

1158

If you are happy, if you are miserable, whether you enjoy every second of life, or if you hate it, it just passes. It is here, then it is gone.

1159

It could never happen to you until it does happen to you.

1160

Suppositions are invalid.

1161

Do you lie?

1162

A collector is never complete within himself.

1163

Is not any type of relationship based on respecting
the other's feelings?

1164

People always speak of, "I will respect your
feelings, if you respect mine" or "What about my
feelings?" If these words are spoken, the person is
not in a relationship. They are simply doing
business and expect a return of their investment.

1165

If one takes each experience in life and does not
place a value judgment of right or wrong, good or
bad upon it, then one is free and not controlled by
remorse or the desire to relive something.

1166

After all the senses are pulled out and drained by
desire, consciousness is the only thing that is left.

1167

Everyone looks at their life and doesn't know where
the time has gone.

That is no consolation, just the truth.

1168

As long as you are living,

       your chances are never over.

1169

What will it prove?

       You never know until you get there.

1170

It does not matter how much you are in the moment,
how much you feel it, how much you live it. For
the moment is gone and life goes by.

1171

Someday you may realize that your pursuits, short-
term desires, and even your occupation added up to
nothing and then you time has all been spent.

1172

Life is like a prison. You are in a cage and society chooses to keep records on you that can never be erased.

1173

Who is greater, the performer for performing or the audience for watching.

1174

If you look for reasons to stay, you will find them.

If you look for reasons to go, you will find them.

1175

Never threaten your opponent with anything, for then they know what to expect and may prepare them self for they know something is coming.

Either do something or do nothing.

Words mean so little.

1176

If you look deep enough into the magic, you will see that it would have happened anyway.

1178

Someday is a long time away.

1179

Any reason is better than no reason at all.

1180

It is interesting how a person claims that another
person's psychic experience was insanity,

       but their own was a realization.

1181

Love is a commodity.

1182

You must make the mundane an exercise in
consciousness, or it will make you go insane.

1183

You have to spend money to get change.

1184

With out a little pain,

       there can be no realization.

1185

You can either choose to love and be peaceful in this moment no matter how bad or uncomfortable it may seem, or you can choose to hate it.

If you choose to love it, you are free. If you choose to hate it, you are miserable.

And, life passes just the same.

1186

You already possess all of the tools necessary to do any needed repairs to yourself, be they physical, mental, or spiritual.

1187

If you give a person hope, they will believe.

1188

There is no way that you can know what you will be like in five years, what your likes will be, what your dislikes will be.

Live for now. Tomorrow will handle itself.

1189

How does one measure life?

1190

Life is a temporary thing.

1191

We are all just sitting here, stuck in the alive
syndrome.

1192

It may be gone, but that is just the chance for
something new to come.

1193

All endings are a beginning.

1194

See it.

1195

In a world where nothing really matters, any dream
will do.

1196

Sit back and feel the perfection.

1197

Life, it does take a lot of time.

1198

The possibilities are endless.

1199

Which side of a peanut butter sandwich is up?

1200

Exist within your own perfection.

Conclusion

Well, as you can see, there are a lot of things one can say about life. Mostly, what I am trying to tell you is that it does not matter what you think or how you feel, for in reality all of our theories are simply that and through time and experience they will change or science will prove them to be wrong. And life, it has no meaning or purpose what-so-ever. So, if you are setting yourself up to believe that you have set out to accomplish something, forget it. Whatever you can or will do can be equally done by another, or in time your endeavors will simply fade away: by nature, new discoveries, or destroyed by the hands of man. A pessimist, no. I am a realist. And come on, nothing is even close to being permanent -- certainly not you or I.

What was the purpose of this book then? Well, it is just my contribution to the nothingness and the illusion that this world is made up of. Sounds some what Zen, huh? This is all simply an exercise in the, *for whatever it is worth.*

I have decided to tie this essence trilogy together, combining the separate texts into one volume; thereby making this the first book that I actually ever began to write. I was fourteen years old. Since that age, it is just something that I do to pass the time between birth and death -- try to figure all of this nonsense out. Just my job, I suppose. It has to be done by someone...

You can probably tell by the growing amount of works per each section that as time has gone on it has become more and more a function of my life to record these little understandings.

Being all that as it may, you will probably see another one of these books issued in a few years, with whatever new realizations I may have come upon. It does take time, you know -- to realize and experience new things and hours upon hours to place them upon paper and organize them into somewhat of a coherent format. Of course, if you are interested in where I am at in the interim, you can always send me a letter.

So live! It is the only advise that I can give you. Take life for whatever it is worth and do not believe in the illusion that it all adds up to something. For it does not.

So, make the experiences your teachers and your loves and your hates your realization. Mostly, just be happy and do not take all of this Life-Stuff so seriously.

Dream on...

S.
26 September 1989
Redondo Beach, California

www.ingramcontent.com/pod-product-compliance
Lightning Source LLC
Chambersburg PA
CBHW062223270326
41930CB00009B/1846